ASP.NET Programming
Success in a Day

By Sam Key

Beginners guide to fast, easy and efficient learning of ASP.NET programming

2nd Edition

Table Of Contents

Introduction

I want to thank you and congratulate you for purchasing the book, "ASP.NET Programming success in a day: Beginners guide to fast, easy and efficient learning of ASP.NET programming ".

This book contains proven steps and strategies on how to do basic programming using the ASP.NET system.

ASP.NET is probably one of the most versatile and yet most often overlooked programming languages today. It offers powerful features, flexibility, and a wide array of options. With later releases, ASP.NET has also begun to significantly develop its cross-platform compatibility, bringing it up to the level of its rival programming languages. Any serious programmer needs to know at least the basics of ASP.NET programming in order to utilize its numerous strong suites -- and this book will help you do just that.

Thanks again for purchasing this book. I hope you enjoy it!

Chapter 1: Intro to ASP.NET

Debunking ASP.NET Myths

If you are into programming languages, you would have surely heard of ASP.NET, Microsoft's open source Web application framework that works server-side. This technology was created to allow programmers to build websites, applications, and web services. Compared to other languages, ASP.NET is fairly new, first released at the start of 2002 with the first version of the company's .NET framework. It is the successor to Microsoft's ASP (Active Server Pages), hence the name.

And if you are into programming languages, you would know that ASP.NET is infamous within the development community. Just like any other platform, the entire .NET system has its own share of valid criticisms. However, .NET has been famous for drawing the ire of more than the usual number of programmers, especially non-users. These are the ones who rely on misconceptions, thinking that ASP.NET is inferior. But most of these are unfounded; just check them out below:

1. **ASP.NET is made by Microsoft, so it should be bad.** Many people think that Microsoft is the big, evil, moneymaking giant of the tech world, and they hate ASP.NET simply for being a Microsoft product. However, it is curious that Google and Apple, two other "evil tech giants" (as many critics call them), have their own programming systems each with a veritable religion of followers. This just proves that so long as the product works well, it should not matter who creates it.

2. **ASP.NET is expensive.** This is perhaps one consistent negative point when ASP.NET is reviewed against other programming languages, but those reviews rarely put the word "expensive" in context. What may be a tad expensive for home users can be extremely cheap if placed in a business environment.

In truth, one of the largest chunks of money spent when developing in ASP.NET is in the cost of Windows itself (provided you are literally starting from scratch and you don't have Windows). In order to stay on top of the game (because alternatives such as the Mono Project lag in development), you could purchase a new machine with an OEM Windows install or purchase a license, which could cost you anywhere from $99 to $189 (the Ultimate edition).

After the Windows install, everything else needed to develop ASP.NET applications (or any .NET applications in general) can be obtained for free. For beginners, Microsoft gives away the WebMatrix integrated development environment (with built-in web server and database engine). For advanced users, an Express (slightly trimmed down) version of Visual Studio is free. And for students, the DreamSpark program makes a lot of MS software available for free.

Finally, Windows hosting has been thought to be much more expensive. This may have held true a decade ago, but there are several reasonably-priced hosting services today (some starting out at $2 per month).

3. **ASP.NET is only for enterprise.** The above point being said, many will cry that ASP.NET is unsuitable for small, personal sites. In fact, one just has to look at the framework's class library to get the feeling. While it's true that some simple things aren't as simple as they should be in .NET and that Microsoft as a platform primarily targeted businesses with the .NET release, they did make a lot of concessions to make the system user-friendly for everyone.

As a first, let us consider the aforementioned WebMatrix for beginners. This offers new developers a simple approach to doing ASP.NET projects. Aside from being very easy to use, it is also created with a simplified API to make things less complex.

Also, ASP.NET offers more than one development approach. In order to create structured programs that can be considered masterpieces of object-oriented design, you can use different methods, even through scripting mentalities that thrive in PHP.

4. **ASP.NET is closed.** While it is easy to assume that Microsoft made this in the same manner that they made any of their other

software, it is surprising to know that the entire ASP.NET system is open source. You can actually step into the code in the process of debugging, and you can even build your personal version of the entire .NET Framework. Even ASP.NET releases such as WebForms and MVC have their codes open.

5. ASP.NET is Windows only. Earlier, we discussed that the main cost in running ASP.NET is in obtaining the Windows OS. However, we also mentioned the Mono Project in the same breath. The Mono Project is a cross-platform version of the ASP.NET, thanks in great part to the openness of the .NET Framework. While not officially supported, the Mono Project has been publicly acknowledged by Microsoft. As mentioned previously, however, Mono is a few steps behind Microsoft's release. This said, it is still growing in popularity -- it even allows programmers to create iOS apps, using the .NET Framework an C#!

6. ASP.NET is not in demand. Many people believe that ASP.NET pales in comparison to other systems such as Javascript, Perl, PHP, Ruby, and about half a dozen more. They reason that ASP.NET is not in demand. Again, this should be put into perspective -- different places have different job markets.

It is worthwhile to note that most Windows software have been developed using the .NET Framework, giving those versed in ASP.NET huge employment opportunities. Mono also factors into this demand -- with the breadth of OS support the Mono Project has, one can write any app for any of the biggest operating systems.

Lastly, consider this: a lot of the most popular websites (including Amazon and eBay) have ASP.NET as their development models. ASP.NET is something big.

Advantages of the ASP.NET Framework

After debunking the common misconceptions against ASP.NET, here are some of the most significant advantages the system has.

ASP.NET Programming Success in a Day 2nd Edition

1. ASP.NET greatly reduces the amount of code that is needed to build larger applications.

2. Built-in Windows authentication (as well as per-application configuration) allows apps developed using ASP.NET to be safe and secure.

3. Early binding, caching services, native optimization, and just-in-time compilation all combine to provide better performance.

4. The ASP.NET framework has a rich designer and toolbox in the VisualStudio IDE. Drag-and-drop server controls, WYSIWYG, automatic deployment, and more are provided by this powerful tool.

5. ASP.NET pages are easy to write and maintain, as the source code and HTML are together. The source code is also executed on the server, providing power and flexibility.

6. The ASP.NET runtime manages and closely monitors the processes, so a new process can be created in case one process is dead. This keeps the application available for handling requests.

7. Being language independent, it allows programmers to choose the languages that best apply to the application. The programmer can also partition the application across different programming languages.

8. There is no need to register components in ASP.NET since configuration is built-in. This makes for easier deployment.

9. The web server implementing ASP.NET closely monitors all pages. Any memory leak, infinite loop, or other illegal activity is immediately destroyed, and the framework restarts itself for continuity.

10. In general, ASP.NET can counter large volumes of users without having performance problems.

Chapter 2: ASP.NET Programming

Those who are used to programming in Classic ASP (circa 1998) need to be reminded that the .NET variant is new generation and is thus not compatible with legacy versions. However, the programming style includes elements of the original.

Pages programmed using ASP.NET, can be distinguished by the extension .aspx. These are usually written in Visual Basic (with the file extension .vbhtml) or C# (.cshtml), though the user controls can be written in C++, Java, and other programming languages.

When the user's browser requests an ASP.NET file, the system's engine reads the file and then compiles and executes the scripts fount. The results are then returned to the user as plain HTML.

Web Pages

Web Pages is actually the name for one of the three programming models used for creating ASP.NET sites and applications (the other two being MVC or Model, View, Controller, and Web Forms). It is the simplest programming model for ASP.NET pages, allowing for a way to easily combine HTML, CSS, Javascript, and other server code. It is built around single web pages so it is easy to understand and use, and it also provides full control over the elements of the page.

MVC, on the other hand, is a little more complicated as it is split into three: the model is the representation of the application core (like the list of records in a database), the view is the data display (such as the records themselves), and the controller is the one handling the input. Like WebForms, it can fully control HTML, CSS, and JavaScript.

Lastly, there is the WebForms which is the oldest programming model in ASP.NET, relying on event-driven pages in a combination of server controls, server code, and HTML. These forms are compiled and ran on the server, which in turn will generate the HTML that will display the web page. Web Forms come with several (hundreds) different controls and other components, meant to build user-driven sites with access to the data.

For simplicity, we will be tackling only Web Pages extensively in this book, as it represents the simplest and most straightforward way of learning ASP.NET.

ASP.NET Razor

The Razor is a new, simple markup syntax that was meant for embedding server code into the web pages. This setup is similar to Classic ASP. The Razor has the same powerful capabilities of the traditional ASP.NET (since it is based on the ASP.NET Framework itself), though it is significantly easier to learn and use. It can be easy to use for beginners, and can drastically the increase the productivity of experts.

Let us suppose that we have the following HTML code for a webpage:

```
<!DOCTYPE html>
<head>
<meta charset= "utf-8" />
<title> Razor Web Pages Sample</title>
</head>
<body>
<h1>Hello World!</h1>
</body>
</html>
```

This page is a very simple one, and we will try adding a Razor code to it:

```
<!DOCTYPE html>
<head>
<meta charset= "utf-8" />
<title> Razor Web Pages Sample</title>
</head>
<body>
<h1>Hello World!</h1>
<p>The time is @DateTime.Now</p>
</body>
</html>
```

The part with Date.Time is the Razor code, which is marked by the "@" sign. This particular code induces the page to display the current date and time. This is done by having the Razor code retrieve the current time on the server. If you want to have other formats, this display can also be customized.

As we mentioned before, there are two languages we can use with these pages -- VB and C#. There are different rules when it comes to using Razor on any of these languages. Here are the ones for C#:

- The blocks of Razor code should always be enclosed in @{...}.

- The inline expressions (i.e. Functions and variables) should always start with an @.

- Code statements should always end with a semicolon (;).

- The **var** keyword is to be used in declaring the variables.

- Quotation marks (" ") should always enclose strings.

- Always remember that the code for C# is case-sensitive.

- Also, remember that the .cshtml extension should be appended to the C# file, or else it would not work as intended.

In contrast, here are the main rules for Visual Basic:

- The blocks of Razor code should always be enclosed by **@Code...End Code**.

- The inline expressions, like in C#, should start with the @ sign.

- The **Dim** keyword is used to declare variables.

- Quotation marks (" ") should always enclose strings.

- The VB code, unlike C#, is not case sensitive.

- The extension .vbhtml is needed for pages done in VB for them to work properly.

Web pages created with Razor can essentially be described as HTML web pages with two different kinds of content: the pure HTML (which you can immediately recognize) and the Razor code which is denoted by the @ sign.

As the page is being read by the server, the Razor code will be run first. Then, ASP.NET will send the HTML page to the browser. The code that the server will execute can do tasks that normally cannot be done in the browser, such as acessing the database. The code from the server will be able to create dynamic content on the spot, right before sending it to the browser. When the browser sees it, it is no different from any other static HTML content

Razor codes can also work with objects, which can be based off text boxes, entire web pages, filed and database records, or they can be self-defined among many other possibilities. There are also objects that have properties describing their characteristics.

Like other programming languages, Razor is also capable of handling "if and else" conditions, as well as reading the user input. These help in the creation of dynamic web pages.

Chapter 3: Creating a Consistent Layout

Web Pages allow a programmer to create content with a consistent look and feel. This means that every site has the same header and footer, and that every page has the same style and layout. This can be done very efficiently, since the programmer can have reusable content blocks (such as the aforementioned headers and footers) in different files. A layout template can also be used to define a consistent layout for all pages.

Content Blocks

Using Web Pages, the programmer can use the **@RenderPage( )** system to import the consistent content from separate files. The content block, which is from another file, can be imported to anywhere within the page. This can contain text, code, and markup just like any other regular webpage.

This saves you a lot of work since you will not have to write the same content in each page. When you change one of the files, the update is carried over to all your pages. Below is an example of how this looks in code:

```
<html>
<body>
@RenderPage("header.cshtml")
<h1>Hello World!</h1>
<p>This is some text</p>
@RenderPage("footer.cshtml")
</body>
</html>
```

In this example, the files "header" and "footer" will be reflected in each page you make. If these files change, the revised files will then be carried over to the pages.

Using a Layout Page

Another approach, as mentioned a little earlier, is using a layout page. This contains only the structure, though it excludes the web page's content. When a layout page is linked to the content itself, then the layout page or template will dictate the display.

The layout page will look just like any other web page, but it includes calling the **@RenderBody( )**. This method will be including the content page. Remember that in this process, the content pages will have to begin with a Layout instruction. Here is how a Layout Page is under the hood:

```
<html>
<body>
<p>This is a header</p>
@RenderBody()
<p>&copy;2015 All Rights Reserved.</p>
</body>
</html>
```

And this is the example of a content page:

```
@{Layout= "Layout.cshtml";}
<h1>Welcome to this webpage!</h1>
<p>Lorem Ipsum</p>
```

Chapter 4: Folders

In the ASP.NET system, there are two different types of folder structures: logical and physical. Below is a set of folders that make up the typical logical folder structure:

- Account. This folder contains all the logon and security files.

- App_Data. This contains all the databases, as well as the data files.

- Images. This folder contains the different images for your page.

- Scripts. These contain the different browser scripts.

- Shared. This folder has all the common files, such as the layout and the style files.

Aside from the logical folder structure which is on your server, there is also the physical location that is on your computer. This should appear familiar:

C:\YourName\Documents\MyWeb\Sample\Images

Virtual versus Physical Names

It is important to distinguish whether the name of a certain item is virtual or physical -- but it's very easy since they just follow the names of the logical/physical folders. For example, a sample image's virtual name may simply be "**Images\sample.png**", while its physical counterpart   is **C:\YourName\Documents\MyWeb\Sample\Images\sample .png**.

Paths and URLS

We know that URLs (Universal Resource Locators) are used to gain access to files and pages from the Web. An example is http://www.yoursite.com/sample/page.aspx.   However,   this corresponds to physical data on the server computer, which is basically just like the physical name in the above section. This is called a "path". The virtual path is made as a shortcut in order to represent the lengthy names of these physical paths. This virtual path is what appears after the ".com" in the above URL: "/sample/page.aspx".

While coding ASP.NET, you will need to make a reference to both the virtual and the physical path, depending on the material is being coded.

ASP.NET provides three different tools for easily working with these folder paths, which will be discussed below:

~ Operator

This specifies the virtual root within the programming code. Using the ~ operator and not the root path will allow you to move the page or site to a different location or folder without changing the code. Below is an example:

```
Var ImagesFolder = "~/images";
Var Style Shet = "~/styles/stylesheet.css";
```

Server.MapPath

This method converts the virtual path (let's say, "/sample.cshtml") into a physical one that can be understood by the server (C:\YourName\Documents\MyWeb\Sample\sample.cshtml).

This method is used when one needs to open the files found on the site's server. It is to be remembered that one can only access data files using a full physical path. An example is shown below:

```
Var pathName = "~/dataFile.txt";
Var fileName = "Server.MapPath(pathName);
```

The next chapter will discuss more about reading and writing data files.

Href

Inherently, the browser cannot understand the ~ operator we have discussed earlier (it is restricted to ASP.NET use only). The Href method can remedy this weakness by converting a path that has been used in the lines of code to a certain path that can be understood by the browser.

The Href style can be used to map out paths to resources such as CSS files and image files. You will use this method frequently in HTML <img>, <link>, and <a> elements. An example is the code below:

```
@{var myStyleSheet = "~/Shared/Layout.css";}
<!-- This is a link to the CSS file: -->
<link rel = "stylesheet" type = "text/css" href = "@Href(myStylesSheet)"/>
<!-- This is the same as: -->
<link rel = "stylesheet| type = "text/css" href = "/Shared/Layout.css" />
```

Chapter 5: Global Pages

Before the Web Startup: _AppStart

Most of the server side codes are written inside the individual web pages. As an example, if a certain page contains any input form, the web page will usually contain server code meant for reading the data.

However, when the programmer creates a page named "_AppStart" in the site's root directory, the startup code can then be executed even before the site starts. If such a page exists, ASP.NET would run it first when any page in the site is requested.

A typical way the _AppStart is used is for startup code and the initialization of global values such as global names and counters.

Note that "_AppStart" should be similar in terms of file extension to the rest of the pages, such as "_AppStart.cshtml" or "_AppStart.vbhtml". Also, note the underscore prefix in "_AppStart". Affixing the underscore to any page will mean that the files contained cannot be directly browsed. This is good since the _AppStart folder usually contains sensitive information.

Before Each Page: _PageStart

In the same way that _AppStart runs even before the site starts, you can also create code that can run even before any page in the folder. For every folder in your site, you can add a file called "_PageStart".

The common use of _PageStart is setting the layout page for each page in the folder. It can also be used to check that a user is logged in before a page is ran.

Basically, when a request for the site and its pages come in, ASP.NET will check whether _AppStart exists. If this is the case and the current request is the first one, _AppStart will run.

Then ASP.NET will check whether the _PageStart document exists. If this is the case, it runs before the page that was requested. If a call to **RunPage( )** inside _PageStart is included, the programmer can specify where the requested page will run. If this is not the case, then _PageStart will run before the requested page.

Chapter 6: HTML Forms

Like in any other programming language, the form is that place in the HTML file where the programmer can put input controls such as radio buttons, check boxes, text boxes, and even drop-down lists.

Below is an example of how to do it, using Razor.

Displaying Images

You can also use Razor in the input field application to dynamically display images according to the user's input.

For example, you would like to use an image named "sample.png" in he image folder of your site. The image can be displayed by using the HTML <img> element such as this:

<img src="images/sample.png" alt="Sample" />

However, if you have three pictures that should be displayed according to the user's options, you can use the following Razor code:

```
<html>
<body>
@{
if (IsPost) {
string username = Request["UserName"];
string email = Request["E-mail"];
<p>You entered: <br />
Company Name: @username <br />
Contact Name: @email </p>
}
else
{
<form method="post" action="">
 UserName:<br />
<input type="text" name="UserName" value="" /><br />
 E-mail Address:<br />
<input type="text" name="email" value="" /><br /><br />
 <input type="submit" value="Submit" class="submit" />
</form>
}
}
</body>
</html>
```

In this example, the server initially forms a variable named the **imagePath**. Then, the HTML points to an input method employing a dropdown list (the <select> element) called **Choice**. This allows the programmer to select a more browser-friendly name (such as "Photo 1"), then relays a file name (such as "sample.png") once the page is submitted to the server.

The code will then read the choice's value by the line **Request["Choice"]**. Once it finds there is a value, the code will construct a path to the file and store this variable in the imagePath.

In any HTML page with an image, an <img> tag is used. The src code is then made to correspond to the value of this imagePath variable once the page loads.

Finally, the <img> element is placed within an "if" block to stop it from attempting to display a nameless image.

Chapter 7: Objects

Up until this point, you have used a few Page Object methods being used. Initially, you had:

```
@RenderPage("header.cshtml")

@RenderBody()
```

And just in the last chapter, you had these lines:

```
If (IsPost) {

if (Request["Choice"] != null) }
```

This chapter will give a better understanding of the different object-related codes.

Page Object Methods

- **Href.** This creates a URL utilizing programmer-specified parameters.

- **RenderBody().** This renders a portion of the content page that is outside any of the named sections (applicable within layout pages).

- **RenderPage(*page*).** This will render a page's content within a different page.

- **RenderSection(*section*).** This will render the content of the named section (applicable within layout pages).

- **Write(*object*).** This will write an object as a string (HTML encoded),

- **WriteLiteral.** This writes an object directly without first encoding it via HTML.

Page Object Properties

- **IsPost.** This returns true when the method of data transfer utilized by the client happens to be a POST.

- **Layout.** This sets or gets the location of the layout page.

- **Page.** This provides access (property-like) to data that is shared between the layout pages and the rest of the pages.

- **Request.** This procures the HttpRequest object and relays it to the existing HTTP request.

- **Server.** This gets the HttpServerUtility object, providing methods of webpage processing

Page Object's Page Property

The page property of a page object will provide a property-like access towards the data being shared between the layout pages and the rest of the content pages. The programmer can add his own properties to the existing Page property:

- Page.Version

- Page.Title

- Page.<insert anything here>

This property can be very helpful -- as an example, it allows the programmer to create the page title in the content files, for use within in the layout file. This is how it appears in a sample "Home.cshtml" page:

```
@{
Layout="~/Shared/Layout.cshtml";
Page.Title="Home Page"
}

<h1>Welcome to this website!</h1>

<h2>Web Site Menu</h2>

<p>Our Home Page (Home.cshtml)</p>
<p>Our Layout (Layout.cshtml)</p>
<p>Our Style Sheet (StyleSheet.css)</p>
```

In contrast, here is how it will look in a sample "Layout.cshtml" website:

```
<!DOCTYPE html>
<html>
<head>
  <title>@Page.Title</title>
</head>
<body>
  @RenderBody()
</body>
</html>
```

Chapter 8: ASP.NET with Text Files

There are times when a programmer wants to access data stored within a text file. These files (also used to store information) are also commonly referred to as "flat files". The common flat file formats include .xml, .txt, and comma-delimited values (.csv).

Displaying Data from the Text File

The text files usually appear in the App_Data folder (hence you need to make one if you want to personally try the following examples). Let's say that you have a new document entitled "Authors.txt" and you have the following content:

Doyle, Arthur Conan

Christie, Agatha

Leblanc, Maurice

This example will show how to show data from this text file:

In this example, Server.MapPath is used to find the exact file path of the text. Then, File.ReadAllLines will open the text document and read all the lines from the text into the array. For every dataItem in all the datalines of these arrays, the data will be displayed.

Showing Data from Excel

Using Microsoft Excel, the programmer can save the spreadsheet as a .csv file. Once this is done, each row in the spreadsheet will be saved and treated like a line of text. Each column will then be separated by a comma, and each row will be saved as a line of text.

The same instruction as mentioned above can read the Excel .csv document-- all you have to do will be to change the filename to the appropriate one.

```
@{
var dataFile = Server.MapPath("~/App_Data/Authors.txt");
 Array userData = File.ReadAllLines(dataFile);
}
<!DOCTYPE html>
<html>
<body>

<h1>Reading Data from a File</h1>
 @foreach (string dataLine in userData)
 {
   foreach (string dataItem in dataLine.Split(','))
   {@dataItem <text> </text>}
   <br />
 }
</body>
</html>
```

Chapter 9: Displaying Information from the Database

Using Web Pages, the programmer will be able to easily show information from a database. Programmers are able connect to any existing database, though this database can be created from scratch. As shown in the following examples, we will be trying to interface with an extant SQL Server Compact database.

Creating a Customers Page

In your folder, let's say that a new file is named "Items.cshtml". You can try using the code below as a replacement for what you have now:

```
@{
var db = Database.Open("SmallShop");
var selectQueryString = "SELECT * FROM Product ORDER BY Name";
}
<html>
<body>
<h1>Small Shop Items</h1>
<table>
<tr>
<th>Id</th>
<th>Product</th>
<th>Description</th>
<th>Price</th>
</tr>
@foreach(var row in db.Query(selectQueryString))
{
<tr>
<td>@row.Id</td>
<td>@row.Name</td>
<td>@row.Description</td>
<td align="right">@row.Price</td>
</tr>
}
</table>
</body>
</html>
```

This example uses the Database.Open(*name*) technique, which connects to the database in two steps:

1. It will search the application's App_Data for the database which will match what is specified in the "name" parameter, with the exception of the filename extension.

2. If the file is not found, it will look for the connection string within the Web.config file of the application. (The connection string is that which shows information about connecting to the database. This may include a name of any SQL database, complete with the username and password, or a file path).

This two-step method will allow the programmer to test out the application with a database, as well as to execute the application on a web host through a connection string.

Chapter 10: ASP.NET Helpers

In ASP.NET, the programmer can take advantage of the use of helpers, which are components that can easily be accessed through single lines of Razor code. Aside from built-in ASP.NET helpers, these can be built in a DIY manner through the Razor syntax, after which they are stored as .cshtml files.

Here is a list of some useful helpers:

- **WebGrid Helper.** This can simplify the display of data, automatically setting up HTML tables and supporting different formatting options. In tip of these, it can also support paging through data as well as sorting by clicking on the headings.

- **Chart Helper.** This can display different types of chart images, with different formatting options and labels. It can also display data from databases, arrays, or files.

- **WebMail Helper.** This will provide functions for sending messages through email, using Simple Mail Transfer Protocol (SMTP).

- **WebImage Helper.** This helper can provide functionality to manage the images in a page. You can also use certain keywords such as watermark, resize, rotate, and flip.

Aside from those mentioned above, the user can also take advantage of third-party helpers to simplify multimedia, social networks, and other components including security and navigation.

These helpers can also be easily installed through WebMatrix. Simply open the Site workspace, click on the Web Pages Administration, log in, and use the search field to look for your desired helpers.

Chapter 11: ASP.NET Debugging

Any application created on any platform can contain a myriad of errors even when it has already been published. While compilation can reliably weed out a lot of the syntax errors, some types of bugs will require the programmer to go through a debugging process. This is the method of examining the code while running so you can verify that both the path and the data fed in are correctly accessed.

The Windows SDK (Software Development Kit) that comes along with ASP.NET contains a Visual Debugger tool that allows the programmer to look at the application's processes as it runs. The tool is called DbgCLR.exe and can be found in the DuiDebug folder of the Microsoft Visual Studio 8\SDK directory. This debugger allows programmers to step through the different statements as they are executed, viewing the data contained in each variable. The Visual Debugger is used by attaching it to the process that will be running the pages of the application. If you are using Internet Information Services versions 5.0 and 5.1 or ISS 6.0 that is running in the version 5.0 application mode, then the process where the Visual Debugger is attached is Aspnet_wp.exe, the worker process for ASP.NET. If you are running version 6.0 of the ISS in worker process isolation mode, however, then you attach the debugger to the W3wp.exe or the thread pool process.

Once a debugger is attached to a specific process, everything that is going on within that process can be seen. On top of this, the debugger will also map the instructions that are executed in the process into the original code. The Visual Debugger has three primary features that help you debug applications they are:

Breakpoints. These are the places within the code when the debugger will send a signal for the application to stop. This will allow you to view the application's state as of that point, and then step through each line.

Stepping. "Stepping through each line" of code is simply running the code line by line. To help make the experience friendlier, Visual Debugger has some iterators that allow the programmer to specify how many times loops will be ran before another stop is reached.

Data Viewing. The debugger also gives different options with regard to the tracking and viewing of data while the application still runs. Modifications to the data can be made once the app stops in a breakpoint, and the application can then be ran again with the modified data.

System Requirements

First of all, for remote debugging, the remote and local computers should be on either a domain or workgroup setup. In order to debug the worker process, the programmer must have the permission to perform the action. By default, an ASP.NET application will run as the ASPNET user. If the worker process is ASPNET or NETWORK SERVICE, then the programmer must have administrative privileges to perform the debugging.

The name of the worker process can change depending on the debugging scenario and version of the IIS. The user account that the worker process runs under can be changed by modifying the machine.config file. This is found on the server that is running the IIS. The best way this is done is to use the IIS Manager. The worker process can also be changed to run under your own user account, and in this case the programmer does not have to be a server administrator to perform the needed actions.

Remember that before changing the worker process so it runs under a different account, it will always be a possibility that the ASP.NET worker process may be hacked when under the new account. The NETWORK SERVICE and ASPNET accounts can run with the minimal permissions, thereby reducing any possible damage taken if the process is hacked. Changing to an account with greater permissions can increase the potential damage.

Configuring Web Apps for Debugging

In order to enable the debugging of ASP.NET Web applications, one must configure the application to be able to compile into a "debug build". This build includes the data that the debugger needs so it can step through the lines of code and display the variables therein. A web app may be configured to use the debug build on the Compilation section of its Web.config file. In case you want to debug individual pages, then the "debug=true" line can be added to the @ Page directive of the relevant pages.

Remember that any application compiled into the debug build may perform a lot more slowly in comparison to the retail build. Before the application is deployed to the market, make sure that the debug mode is turned off. Debug mode also causes more information to be exposed in the stack once an error occurs, which can potentially mean a security issue for the product.

Remote and Local Debugging

A web server that s locally run (such as IIS) can allow you to debug applications locally running on your computer. These pages can then be viewed in a browser.

However, when a page cannot be run locally due to the inability to run a Web Server (or simply because the app is not locally available), then a remote debug can be performed. In order to do this, Virtual Studio's remote debugging components must be installed on the remote server.

Debugging Permissions

The process of debugging requires more privileges than simply running the same app. In addition to securing configurations in the app for debugging, it is also mandatory that there are adequate permissions secured to allow the attaching of the debugger to the relevant process. Users will have the permission to debug local processes running under their credentials, but another user's processes will not be accessible to them for debugging.

Administrators, on the other hand, can access and debug any process by any user.

The same thing goes when you are debugging on a remote server, as you will need the admin privileges of the computer where the process runs.

Client-Side Script Debugging

In addition to the application debugging done on the server side, Visual Debugger also lets you debug the client script as long as it is written on JavaScript (EMCAScript) or VBScript. This feature can be especially useful when the programmer has Web server controls using client-side scripts.

Debugging Deployed Web Apps

You might need to debug a web application that has already been running on a production server. This is possible, but it should be done with caution. Let's say that you have attached the worker process of ASP.NET for debugging, and a breakpoint has been hit. This will cause all the managed code in the worker process to halt. Halting these managed codes, in turn, can cause a stoppage to all the work for all users on the specific server. It is important to understand the impact to the production in case you decide to debug on a production server.

Aside from adding the debugger to the relevant ASP.NET worker process, double check that the Visual Debugger is given access to the application's symbols. The source files for the application also need to be located and opened.

A lot of the ASP.NET applications will reference DLLs containing business logic or some other useful bits of code. These references automatically copy the DLLs from the local computer to the \bin folder in the virtual directory of the Web app. When debugging, remember that the application will be referencing this and not the local copy on the computer.

The methods used for attaching the worker process to the debugger are the same as those of other remote processes. When the attachment is successful, not opening the correct project will leave you with a dialog box when the application reaches a breakpoint. This box will ask for the location of the source files. The filename which is specified in this box must be the same filename specified in the debug symbols of the server.

Enabling Debugging for ASP.NET Web Applications

To enable the debugging option, one must enable this both in the Project Properties menu and the web configuration file of the application. Note that the commands and dialog boxes that you see can differ from those listed in Help documentations, depending on the software edition or your current settings. The settings can be changed by choosing "Import and Export" in your Tools menu.

Enabling in Project Properties

1. Go to Solution Explorer and right-click your project s name. From the options, select "Properties".

2. Under the Properties menu, click on the tab marked "Web".

3. Select ASP.NET from the debuggers option.

Enabling using web.config file

1. Open web.config using any XML parser or web editor. Note that this cannot be accessed remotely using your web browser. By default, the Microsoft IIS is configured to prevent browsers from directly accessing the Web.config file. This is for security purposes. Accessing the configuration file through a browser will get you an "Access Error 403 (Forbidden)".

2. Since the configuration file is written in XML, it will contain nested sections that are marked using"tags. Find the element that says "configuration/system.web/compilation". In case this element is"non-existent, you will have to manually create it.

3. In case the aforementioned element did not have any debug

attribute, this will also have to be manually added.

4. Make sure that once the attribute of the debug is added, its value is changed to "true".

Here is an example of how the web configuration file would look like:

```
<configuration>

    ...

    <system.web>

        <compilation

            Debug="true"

                ...

        >

        ...

        </compilation>

    </system.web>

</configuration>
```

Robust Programming

The programming language will automatically detect all changes made to the configuration files, and these changes will automatically be applied in the settings. Thus, the programmer no longer has to reboot the IIS server or the computer for the changes to appear.

Another good aspect of ASP.NET is that it inherits the settings from the config files found higher up the URL hierarchy. This is especially useful since a site can contain more than one multiple directories and subdirectories stored virtually, with each one possibly containing a web.config file. However, in case the debug was set on any file lower down the hierarchy, the higher debug value will be overridden.

Let's say that you specified the "debug=true" value in www.yoursite.com/file/web.config, then any application within the "file" folder and in all its subfolders would inherit the mentioned setting. So when the application you are looking for is located in the /file/file2 folder, it will inherit the setting in the "file" folder. The exception is when one of these applications override the config setting through its own web.config.

Chapter 12: Monitoring the Health of ASP.NET Applications

Health monitoring is a task that ensures that the application is healthy. Any failing systems will be rapidly diagnosed, and significant events that happen during the application's life cycle can be appraised. ASP.NET applications can be monitored either individually or across a "Web farm", and the monitoring can be configured not just errors but also events that happen within the app.

The health monitoring system built into ASP.NET includes event types that work by packaging the application's health status information. There are also provider types that serve to process the information about the event. These listen for the events and consume the information, usually through logging the info or by sending a notification to the administrator. Connecting an event to a provider (commonly referred to as "enabling an event") is done by making the settings in the config files. And then, there are the additional types that help in managing these events.

The health monitoring system of ASP.NET is implemented through the classes found in the namespace "System.Web.Management".

Configuring Monitoring

ASP.NET apps can be configures to use customized or built-in monitoring tools. Providers and web events can be added to the app through the "healthMonitoring" section of the config file. After accessing this, the programmer can use different classes for the processing of the data.

Class Hierarchy: Web Events

When the event is raised, an associated event class will be raised. Data about the event will be collected in the object's properties, which are in turn processed by the event providers.

These events can contain a myriad of information, such as those coming from audit events, configuration errors, application errors, response data, request data, application domain, and worker process.

Health information contained in the parent event class will be inherited by child event classes. The further down in the hierarchy of Web event classes an event is, the more specific to the application the data is. Derived classes can, for example, expose information like client IPs, stack traces, and process and thread information.

Class Hierarchy: Providers

● The built-in providers can be used to process the Web events. A programmer can also inherit from these built in classes to create custom providers. These, however, are subject to the following limitations of inheritance:

● The class WebEventProvider can be inherited by apps running under any trust level.

● The class BufferedWebEventProvider can be inherited by apps running under any trust level.

● The class SqlWebEventProvider can be inherited by apps running under Full trust.

● The other classes cannot be inherited by the apps, no matter the trust level.

Using Built-in Providers and Web Events

This is the most common strategy in the use of health monitoring tools. The only requirement will be to configure the application to use the items you will need. There are a few tasks you will have to perform first:

● Add the web event class you will need to the element "eventMappings" of the "healthMonitoring" section of the app's configuration file.

● Add to the provider's element (found in the healthMonitoring section) the provider which consumes the event.

- Add to the rules element an item that defines the association between the provider and event.

In the default settings, the built-in classes can be configured in the healthMonitoring segment of the root config file. The following default configurations are established by the section:

Specify in eventMappings the web event classes deriving from WebBaseEvent. This section can be used to assign friendly names to any group of event classes.

Include in at least one of the aforementioned defined groups the event classes deriving from the WebBaseEvent.

In the providers element, the following event providers are specified: EventLogWeEventProvider, SqlWebEventProvider, and WmiWebEventProvider. The programmer can specify other built-in providers in the providers element, like TemplatedMailWebEventProvider, SimpleMailWebEventProvider, and TraceWebEventProvider.

The rules associating the audit failure events and Web error to EventLogWebEventProvider classes are detailed in the element "rules". You may enable Web events and providers by appending to the rules elements. Any event will be considered enabled if this is mapped to any event provider in this element. The provider and eventMappings elements need to be configured for the event, and unless the two will be connected in the rules element, the event will not be enabled.

The programmer can also detail the parameter values for configured items. These examples include parameters limiting the number of occurring events, those specifying the interval between different events, or those specifying the SQL and mail providers buffering options.

Chapter 13: Displaying Safe Error Messages

When the app displays errors, it must not be in such a manner that vulnerable information is given out as this can be used by a malicious attacker to hack or jeopardize your system. As an example, if the application attempts to unsuccessfully log into a database, the error message must not display the username that is being used.

There are different means to control the error messages shown to the users, and this includes the following:

- Configuring the app to not give out verbose errors to the remote users. These "Remote Users" refer to those who request for the app's pages while not on a computer connected directly to the server. These errors can optionally be redirected to an app page.

- Error handling can be included whenever possible, and your own version of error messages may also be constructed. In the error handler, the programmer may test to check whether this specific user is a local one. If so, the system can react accordingly.

- Global error handlers can be created at the application or page level. This catches all the unhanded exceptions, routing them to a more generic page showing a customer error message. This way, even when a problem is not anticipated, users won't be seeing any exception page.

Configuring applications to disallow the error messages for the remote users

Tweaking the web configuration file for the specific application, the following modifications can be made to your customErrors:

- Setting the mode to RemoteOnly. Remember, this is case-sensitive. The change will configure the app to show the detailed errors when the user is local -- specifically, if the developer tries to connect to the app.

- Put up defaultRedirect attributes that will be pointing to the app error page.

- Put an <error> element that will redirect some specific instances to some specific pages. As an example, a standard "Page not found" (404) error message can be found on the app page.

The following codes show an example of what the usual customErrors block looks like in a Web.config.

```
<customErrors                                    mode="RemoteOnly"
defaultRedirect="AppErrors.aspx">

    <error statusCode="404" redirect="NoSuchPage.aspx"/>

    <error statusCode="403" redirect="NoAccessAllowed.aspx"/>

</customErrors>
```

Including Error Handling

First, place try-catch blocks around statements that could generate an error. You may also optionally check with local users having the IsLocal, then modify the error handling. The value equivalent to the localhost is 127.0.0 – this means that the web browser is running on the same PC as the server.

The following lines show an example of the error-handling block. When an error appears, then a session state variable will be loaded with the message details. The application will then display a page which will be able to read your Session variable, as well as subsequently display your error message. These error messages will be those specifically written to not provide exploitable items to another user. For local users, a different set of error details can be provided. Within your "finally" block, we will release an open resource.

```
Try
{
    sqlConnection1.Open();
    sqlDataAdapter1.Fill(dsCustomers1);
}
Catch (Exception ex)
{
    If(Request.IsLocal)
    { Session["CurrentError"] = ex.Message}
    Else
    { Session["CurrentError"] = "Error processing page.;}
    Server.Transfer("ApplicationError.aspx");
}
Finally
{
    this.sqlConnection1.Close();
}
```

Creating Global Error Handlers

A programmer can also make error handlers that can catch all the different unhandled exceptions within page level and even at the application level in full.

To make these global handlers, simply make one for your System.Web.UI.TemplateControl.Error. Application-wide handlers are separately handled within the Global.asax data – simply add the code to your System.Web.HttpApplication.Error. These will be called if unhandled exceptions occur within the application or page. Additional information regarding the latest error can be obtained from GetLastError.

Note that if you already have global error handlers, it will take precedence over the error handling methods specified within the attribute "defaultRedirect", in the "customErrors" config element.

Here is an example (in code) of how a handler gets information regarding the error, places it within the Session variable, then calls an error-handling option which in turn extracts and displays the information on the error.

```
Protected void Application_Error(Object sender, EventArgs e)
{
    Session["CurrentError"] = "Global: "
        Server.GetLastError().Message;
    Server.Transfer("lasterr.aspx");
}
```

Chapter 14: ASP.NET Security

How Security Works

After creating your application, you have to make sure that your website is secured. This is a common complex issue for Web developers, especially since today's Internet landscape is rife with vulnerabilities waiting to be exploited by those with less than noble intentions. A site's protection requires careful plans to be put in place, and a programmer or administrator needs to have a clear understanding in the options needed to secure the site.

The ASP.NET system works hand in hand with Microsoft's .NET framework and the IIS (Internet Information Services) to help provide web app security. This means that the programmer or administrator will also have access to the built-in security capabilities of the framework. This includes code access security as well as role-based security. The IIS can also grant or revoke access based on the IP address or host name of a user. Further authorization steps will have to be performed through URL authentication of the NTFS file access permission.

In protecting your application, you need to utilize the two primary functions of ASP.NET security -- authentication and authorization.

Authentication

Authentication is essentially the verification process undertaken to ensure that the user is really who he says he is. The app will obtain credentials, including the name, password, or various other forms of identification and will perform validation on them against an established authority. Once the credentials are found to be valid, the entity (user, computer) that submitted those credentials will be considered "authenticated".

Once authenticated, the entity will then be checked for access rights to a particular resource. In ASP.NET, authentication is provided through the use of authentication providers, code modules that will have the code necessary to authenticate the credentials of those who made access requests.

First among these is the Windows Authentication provider, which will treat the identity supplied by the IIS as the user which is authenticated in the application. By default, the IIS will provide a number of authentication methods such as Windows integrated (NTLM) authentication, anonymous authentication, Windows integrated (Kerberos) authentication, Digest authentication, Basic (or Base64 encoded) authentication, and even authentication that is based on client certificates.

On the other hand, there are forms of authentication providers that enable the app owner to authenticate users via the name and password, which are submitted through a login form that is created by the programmer. Requests that are not authenticated by the previous means will be redirected to this login page, where the user submits the information through the form. Once the app authenticates the request, the system will issue a key (through a ticket) that establishes the identity for the subsequent requests.

Authorization

On the other hand, authorization is the process which will limit the access granted (or denied) to a specific user, coinciding with his permissions even as an authenticated authority.

There are also two ways to perform authorization. First is the File authorization, which is performed using the FileAuthorizationModule. This will check the ACL (access control list) of the handler file (either .aspx or .asmx) to determine whether the user should gain access to that file. The ACL permissions determine this as well.

There is also URL authorization, which is performed through the UrlAuthorizationModule. This maps the users and the roles to the different URLs within the ASP.NET applications. This module can then be used to selectively allow or deny a person access to any arbitrary part of the application, usually directories, for different roles.

Through the URL Authorization feature, an administrator can explicitly allow or block a user from getting to specific place in the directory based solely on a predetermined role or by assigning this access to the username. The permissions that are established for the directory will also be inherited by the subdirectories, unless a separate subdirectory configuration will override them.

Show below is the syntax for the code in the authorization section:

<authorization>

  <[allow|deny] users role verbs />

</authorization>

In the aforementioned code, the allow or deny segment is a must. The programmer needs to specify either the roles or users attributes; though it is not required to put both of them at once, it can be done. Likewise, the verbs attribute is an optional one.

As is obvious, placing either the allow or deny elements will either grant or revoke the access. Each element will support the rest of the attributes. Users will target the user accounts or identities. In this case, anonymous users will be identified using a question mark. All authenticated users can be specified through the use of an asterisk. The roles will serve to identify the RolePrincipal object for the specific request that will either be allowed or denied access to the resource. Lastly, the verbs will define the HTTP verbs applying to the action. This includes "get", "head", and "pos". The default is an asterisk, which specifies all the verbs.

Below is an example code that will grant access to an identity named "Chris", and the members of the Admin role. The code will also deny access to "Erick", (unless this identity is included in the admin group), as well as to all anonymous users.

```
    <allow users="Chris"/>
    <allow roles="Admins" />
    <deny users="Erick"/>
    <deny users="?"/>
</authorization>
```

The following code, on the other hand, will show how to allow Erick access to the system and deny the same access to everybody else.

```
<authorization>
    <allow users="Erick"/>
    <deny users="*"/>
</authorization>
```

Multiple entities may be specified for both the roles and users attributes, through a comma-separated list. Below is an example:

```
<allow users="Chris, Erick, contoso\Jam"/>
```

Note that if a domain account name is specified, then the name should have both the username and the domain (hence, contoso\Jam).

Below is another example that will allow users to perform HTTP GET for a certain resource, but only the name Chris will be allowed to perform POST.

```
<authorization>

    <allow verbs="GET" users="*"/>

    <allow verbs ="POST" users="Kim"/>

    <deny verbs="POST" users="*"/>

</authorization>
```

There are also rules that apply here. First, the rules contained in the application-level configuration files will take precedence over any inherited rules. The system will determine which rule will take precedence through the construction of a combined list of all the rules for a URL, including the most recent rules (or those nearest in the hierarchy) towards the head of this list.

Also, given a set of combined rules for the app, ASP.NET will start at the head of the list and will check the rules until it finds the first match. The default config of the ASP.NET will contain an element (<allow users="*">) which will authorize all users, though this is also applied last. If no other rules will match, then the request will be allowed. On the other hand, if the match found is a "deny" rule, then the request will return the 401HTTP status code. Of course, a matching "allow" element will let the request proceed.

Within the config file, the location element can also be created to specify a particular directory or file that will be the object of the settings of the location element.

Chapter 15: General Security Practices for ASP.NET

There are sometimes when new programmers attempt to secure their apps with elaborate measures, but fail to cover the simplest ways malicious attackers can get into their system. The following tips will prove not only easy but also effective in maintaining the integrity of your ASP.NET application.

1. Aside from backing up often, make sure that the backup devices are physically stored in a secure place.

2. Keep the Web server PC secured as well so that it cannot be accessed in any way by unauthorized users.

3. Use the NTFS file system instead of FAT32. The Windows file system can offer more security than its counterparts.

4. Secure not just the web server but also all the other computers in your network with strong passwords. If possible, use a different password for each one.

5. Secure your IIS.

6. Close off any unused ports and turn off any services that are not being used.

7. Use an anti-virus app that offers real-time monitoring of inbound and outbound traffic.

8. Establish and enforce policies forbidding the users from writing down their passwords in easy-to-find locations.

9. Use firewalls. Microsoft offers advice and guidelines on the different types of firewalls that should be sued for different systems and applications.

10. Always install security patches from Microsoft and third-part vendors. Microsoft's site has a list of all the latest security updates and other safety bulletins.

11. Utilize the event logging features of Windows, and check the logs regularly to ensure that suspicious activity can be detected as soon as possible. Any repetitive attempts to log onto the system and abnormally high numbers of requests against the server should raise a red flag.

Running Applications with Minimal Privileges

When the apps run, they run within a context of specific privileges on the local device and also possibly on the remote computers. In order to run with the least possible of these privileges, make sure not to run your app with the administrator (system user) identity. Always set permissions (ACLs) on the resources required for the application using the least permissive settings. As an example, if it will not cause your app to malfunction, set all files to be read-only.

Also, keep all the files of the app in a folder located below the root. Never allow your users an option to specify the path for the access of any file. This technique will help prevent users from getting to the server's root.

Knowing your Users

For most apps available online, users can access the site without the need to provide credentials. If this is the case, your app accesses the resources it needs by running as a predefined user. On Windows 2000 or XP, this is defaulted to the local ASPNET user context (for later versions, it is the NETWORK SERVICE) on the server PC.

If your app is in an intranet, restrict the access to authenticated users by configuring the app to use the Windows Integrated Security. This way, the logon credentials of the user can be used to access resources. This is also called impersonation.

If you will need to gather the credentials from the user, use one of the authentication strategies described above.

Guarding Against Malicious Input

To be safe, assume the general rule that the input you receive from the users is never safe. It will be very easy for malicious users to send dangerous information from the client facing them to the app itself. To guard against this eventuality, make sure to follow the following guidelines:

1. In the Web Pages, make sure to check for HTML tags by filtering the user input. Such tags can contain malicious scripts.

2. Never display or echo the unfiltered input. Before displaying this, process the HTML to turn the scripts into strings for display.

3. If you want to accept HTML as a user input, make sure to filter it manually. This will let you define what part of the input will be accepted. This is better than creating a filter that explicitly tried to filter the malicious code, as it will be practically impossible to make sure that all eventualities are anticipated and taken care of.

4. Never assume that the information coming from the HTTP request header is safe. This is in the HttpRequest object. Apply safeguards for cookies, query strings, and the like. Beware of any information that the browser will report to the server, as this can be spoofed when that can be important to the application.

5. If at all possible, never store the sensitive information somewhere that can be accessed from the browser. This can include cookies and hidden fields. As an example, never store passwords in cookies.

The view state will be stored in an encoded format, in a hidden field. By default, this will include a message authentication code or MAC, which allows the page to determine whether the view state has been tampered with. If a sensitive information is stored in the view state, you should encrypt it by setting the ViewStateEncryptionMode to true.

Accessing the Databases Securely

Usually, the databases have their own level of security. This is an important aspect of secure web applications, including the designing of a way for the app to securely access the database.

To ensure this, make sure that the inherent database security is accessible only to limited people. The strategy can change according to your application. For example, if it will not cause your app to fail, you can use integrated security so users who are Windows-authenticated can access the database. This is more secure than passing the credentials to the database. On the other hand, if the app involves allowing users to access it anonymously, then creating a single user with minimal permissions and doing queries while connected as this user can help check security.

Also, remember not to create SQL statements through concatenated strings involving user input. Create instead a parameterized query and use the aforementioned user input to set the parameter values.

If a username and password must be stored somewhere for use as credentials for database login, store them within the web.config file. Encrypt this in turn with protected configuration.

Keeping Sensitive Information

Aside from system information and the like, there may also be information that you wish to keep private. Any of info of this kind should be considered "sensitive" information. This may range from passwords and encryption keys to notes about your application. If anyone gets to this, then your application can be compromised.

If the app will transmit any sensitive information at all between the server and the browser, then consider the use of SSL (Secure Sockets Layer). The Microsoft knowledge base gives a lot of information on this.

You can also use a form of protective configuration in order to secure this information. Make sure as well not to keep this info in a web page, even in any form (such as the server code) that you will not expect people to see.

In the namespace System.Security.Cryptography, strong algorithms for encryption are supplied. These can be used to your advantage as well.

Using Cookies Securely

Cookies can be very useful in keeping user-specific data available. However, because they also get sent to the computer running the browser, they can be spoofed or used for other malicious means. Remember to never install any critical information on these cookies, such as passwords, even momentarily. As a rule of thumb, anything on a cookie that can compromise the app should not be in a cookie in the first place. Instead of the info itself, keep a reference in the cookie that points to the server location of this data.

Remember as well to set expiration dates on cookies. These should be in the shortest time practical. If it will not break the app, never use permanent cookies. As an added measure, consider adding an encryption to the info in the cookies. Setting the HttpOnly and Secure properties of the cookie to the value "true" can also help.

Guarding Against DDOS

DDOS or Denial of Service is a malicious attack that makes your system unavailable for use by other people. This is done by overloading your server with requests, therefore keeping it too busy. In the worst case, this can crash the application.

You can use different error handling techniques such as try-catch. Like mentioned above, you can use a "finally" block so you can release the resources when the app fails.

Process throttling may also be configured for use by the IIS, preventing the app from hogging the CPU time. Size limits of the user input can be tested before they are used or stored. Safeguards can also be placed on the queries -- as an example, before query results are displayed in the ASP.NET Web page, you should first be sure that there is not an unreasonable amount of records.

Putting a limit on the allowable upload size should also be a part of the app. The following syntax can be used (varying the maxRequestLength in kilobytes:

```
<configuration>
  <system.web>
    <httpRuntime maxRequestLength="4096" />
  </system.web>
</configuration>
```

The RequestLengthDiskThreshold property may also be used to reduce the overhead (in memory) of large forum posts and uploads.

Aside from the different risks encountered in this chapter, you should also be familiar with other app security threats so you can wisely defend against them. Remember that secure technology is but a part of the overall solution.

Four of the more common but less defended threats are as follows:

1. **Repudiation.** This is a threat that involves entering into a transaction in such a way that there is no proof of those truly involved afterwards. This can mean impersonating the credentials of an innocent user. To guard against this, you need to have stringent authentication in place.

2. **Elevation of privilege.** This is a type of attack that takes advantage of malicious means to get more permission that what has been normally assigned. A good example is a user being able to secure administrative privileges, therefore giving that user access to all data on the server. This can also lend the user control over the server's capabilities. A minimal privilege context is an effective means to battle this type of attack, as discussed before.

3. **Tampering.** This type of attack refers to the deletion of a resource without proper authorization. An example is the defacing of a

webpage, where the user gets into the site and changes the files therein. Script exploits are common vehicles of this type of attack. These scripts, as discussed above, can enter your app through the use of an input field.

4. **Information Disclosure.** This is simply stealing and/or revealing the information that was supposed to be secure and private. A very common example is stealing login credentials like passwords, though this can extend to any type of file in the entire system. A good way to prevent this from happening is to avoid having passwords and other information to store in the first place. Cryptographic techniques such as storing hashes help greatly in making sure that the information, even if stolen, would be completely useless to the hacker.

Conclusion

Thank you again for purchasing this book!

I hope this book was able to help you to learn the ropes of basic ASP.NET programming.

The next step is to actually start programming your ASP.NET pages! Remember that this book only tackled the beginning. There are several different topics under ASP.NET, just like in any other programming language. Make sure to study and practice so that you will be on your way to making your ASP.NET masterpiece!

Finally, if you enjoyed this book, please take the time to share your thoughts and post a review on Amazon. We do our best to reach out to readers and provide the best value we can. Your positive review will help us achieve that. It'd be greatly appreciated!

Thank you and good luck!

Check Out My Other Books

Below you'll find some of my other popular books that are popular on Amazon and Kindle as well. Simply click on the links below to check them out. Alternatively, you can visit my author page on Amazon to see other work done by me.

C Programming Success in a Day

Android Programming in a Day

C ++ Programming Success in a Day

Python Programming in a Day

PHP Programming Professional Made Easy

CSS Programming Professional Made Easy

Windows 8 Tips for Beginners

If the links do not work, for whatever reason, you can simply search for these titles on the Amazon website to find them.

www.ingramcontent.com/pod-product-compliance
Lightning Source LLC
Chambersburg PA
CBHW071000180526
45168CB00003B/1228